ENDANGERED GRASSLAND ANIMALS

Dave Taylor

Crabtree Publishing Company

ENDANGERED ANIMALS SERIES

Text and photographs by Dave Taylor

For Anne

Editor-in-chief
Bobbie Kalman

Editors
Janine Schaub
Shelagh Wallace

Type output
Lincoln Graphics

Design and computer layout
Antoinette "Cookie" DeBiasi

Color separations
ISCOA

Cover mechanicals
Diane Coderre

Printer
Worzalla Publishing

Published by
Crabtree Publishing Company

350 Fifth Avenue	6900 Kinsmen Court	73 Lime Walk
Suite 3308	P.O. Box 1000	Headington
New York	Niagara Falls, ON	Oxford OX3 7AD
N.Y. 10118	Canada L2E 7E7	United Kingdom

Cataloguing in Publication Data
Taylor, Dave, 1948-
    Endangered grassland animals

(The Endangered animals series)
Includes index.
ISBN 0-86505-528-9 (library bound) ISBN 0-86505-538-6 (pbk.)

1. Grassland fauna - Juvenile literature.
2. Endangered species - Juvenile literature.
3. Wildlife conservation - Juvenile literature.
I. Title. II. Series: Taylor, Dave, 1948-
The endangered animals series.

QL115.T38 1992   j591.52'909153

Contents

The grasslands of the world

A wide variety of animals make their homes in grassland areas. Grasslands offer an abundance of food for millions of creatures. About 8,000 species of grasses grow on the grasslands of the world, feeding large herds of animals.

What is a grassland?

Grasslands can be found on every continent except Antarctica. No matter where they are, these areas have several things in common. All grasslands are grassy. Some have short grasses that can survive without rain; others have grasses that are taller than an elephant and need a lot of rain. Grasslands are usually found on gently rolling hills or flat, level plains. They are dry for part of the year and are almost always windy.

Food for animals and humans

Grasslands feed thousands of species of animals, but human beings like to eat grasses, too. We grow grasses such as wheat, oats, barley, rye, rice, and corn. These varieties of grasses are used to make bread, cereal, pasta, alcohol, and all kinds of desserts and snacks.

Not enough land or food

There are more people in the world today than ever before—and the population is rapidly growing. That means that people need more land on which to live and grow food. As people use more land, there is less land for animals, and fewer animals are able to stay alive. Today only small areas of the world are left on which wild animals can still graze.

Learning and caring

Many grassland animals are in danger of becoming extinct because they are losing their **habitats**. The best way to help these animals is by learning and caring about them and supporting conservation groups who are working hard to preserve endangered animals. Reading about the grasslands and their wondrous inhabitants is a great way to start!

There are many different names for grasslands. In Europe and Asia they are called **steppes;** *in North America they are known as* **prairies** *or* **plains.** **Pampas** *is the South American name for grasslands, and* **veld** *and* **savanna** *are names for grasslands in Africa. The bison below are grazing on the plains.*

Animals in distress

In recent years, people have forced many kinds of animals to struggle for survival. Hunting, farming, and the loss of wilderness areas have made life difficult and sometimes impossible for thousands of species of animals.

Worldwide conservation groups have developed various terms to describe animals in distress. Animals that are **extinct** have not been seen in the wild for over fifty years. Animals referred to as **endangered** are likely to die out if their situation is not improved. **Threatened** animals are endangered in some areas where they live. **Rare** animals are species with small populations that may be at risk.

There is a concern for all animals living in the wild. Even if some species are not yet threatened or endangered, they may lose their lives because of pollution or loss of their homes. There is hope, however. Due to the efforts of conservation groups, many animals that once faced extinction are now surviving in healthy numbers again.

Cheetahs are losing their natural habitats because people need the land on which these cats live for farming. Although cheetahs are protected in most countries, not everyone obeys the laws that make it illegal to hunt them. Farmers sometimes shoot hungry cheetahs that kill small farm animals. The problems of cheetahs are shared by other grassland animals. Wild animals cannot compete with people for land. They always end up losing!

The white rhinoceros

In the past twenty-five years, the rhinoceros population has dropped by eighty-five percent. There are five species of rhinoceros remaining in the world, and they are all endangered. The white rhino is the largest of all the rhinoceros species. It is also the most numerous. About 5,000 live in the wildlife reserves of the African countries of South Africa and Zimbabwe.

Living in small herds

White rhinos feed on growing grass. They are called **grazers**. Their mouths are long and square and resemble the mouths of cows. These large mouths allow rhinos to bite off big bunches of grass all at once. Like most grazers, white rhinos live in herds of five to ten individuals. The herd is made up of mothers and their female calves.

A mother rhino carries her baby for sixteen months. After the baby rhino, called a calf, is born, it stays with its mother for approximately four years. If the calf is a male, it will then leave or be chased away by its mother. If it is a female, it may stay with its mother's herd until the mother gives birth to another calf. Then the female calf will live nearby on its own but still remain part of the herd.

*A rhinoceros can turn its ears to hear sounds coming from any direction. The rhino's horns are not made of ivory—they are made of **keratin**, a tissue found in our fingernails and hair. The white rhino has a keen sense of smell and hearing, but it cannot see very well.*

Dangerous poachers

In the wild, lions and hyenas are the rhino's only natural enemies. Sometimes these **predators** kill and eat rhino calves, but the rhino herd is very good at protecting its young. On the other hand, the white rhino has very little defense against people. Even though it is against the law, there are plenty of people, called **poachers**, who hunt rhinos illegally. They risk going to jail and even losing their lives for a rhino horn.

Poachers take these risks because a rhino horn can sell for as much as $40,000. The horns are ground up and used to make medicines by people in Asian countries. They are also bought to be fashioned into special dagger handles by the people of North Yemen. The dagger, called a **jambia**, is the national symbol of this country. It is given to every young man when he reaches manhood. Although it is now against the law to bring rhino horns into North Yemen, some people feel that it is their sacred tradition to give their sons jambias made from rhino horns.

Desperate measures

Many countries now provide armed guards to protect the remaining white rhinos. This extreme measure has so far saved the majestic white rhino from extinction.

Height: 63-73 inches (160-185 centimeters)
Length: 145-160 inches (368-406 centimeters)
Weight: Up to 3 tons (2722 kilograms)
Where it lives: African grasslands

The pronghorn

In the 1800s, the prairies and plains of North America were home to nearly fifty million pronghorn. When the settlers moved west, they started farming the lands on which the pronghorn lived. Thousands upon thousands of these animals were killed for food and for their skins. Before long, the huge herds were gone. By 1925 there were only 13,000 left.

Today, thanks to conservation laws and protected areas, pronghorns are once again running free on the American plains. They still face the same problems faced by many other grassland animals, however. Their habitats are constantly shrinking.

The pronghorn is a true North American species. It has the features of both a goat and an antelope, but it is neither of these animals.

A unique animal

Although this animal is sometimes called a "pronghorn antelope," it is not an antelope at all. It is a unique animal. The pronghorn is the only existing member of a family of animals that was once common in North America. All the other members of this family died out thousands of years ago but, somehow, the pronghorn survived. There is no other animal quite like it on earth today.

Shedding their horns

Pronghorns are the only horned animals that shed their horns each year. All other horned animals, such as cows, antelope, sheep, and goats, have horns that grow bigger every year but never fall off.

Speedy runners

Pronghorns are the fastest land animals in North America. They can run as fast as 55 miles (89 kilometers) per hour. Scientists wonder why pronghorns are able to run so quickly because they have no enemies that can chase them that fast. Perhaps in the past there was a predator that could catch them, but this animal no longer exists.

Does and fawns

Pronghorns live in herds made up of **does** and **fawns**. The does, or female pronghorns, usually have twin babies, called fawns. When the fawns are four days old, they can run faster than a human. They cannot run as far as their parents, so they must hide from their predators until they are able to outrun them.

Height: 34 inches (86 centimeters)
Length: 55 inches (140 centimeters)
Weight: 103-150 pounds (47-68 kilograms)
Where it lives: Western United States and Canada and northern Mexico

Male pronghorns try to defend a large area of land with food on it so that the females will come onto it and mate. This land is called their "territory." If two males meet on these patches of land, they fight, pushing each other back and forth with their horns locked until one gives up and runs away.

Bison live in herds of twenty to fifty animals. The adult herd animals, which are all female, rank themselves from strongest to weakest. They use shoving matches to find the leader.

The bison of North America

When the European settlers first saw the bison, they mistakenly called it a buffalo. Today many people still call these mighty animals by the wrong name. Bison are very different from buffalo. They have smaller horns and much larger shoulders. Buffalo are found in Africa, Australia, and Asia, whereas bison are found in Europe and North America. Historians think that there may have been over sixty million bison roaming the North American plains two hundred years ago.

Bison live in small herds

People used to believe that huge herds of bison lived together. In fact, a typical bison herd is made up of twenty to fifty animals. The adults are usually all females, called cows. In the summertime, however, the males, or bulls, join the herd to mate with the cows. For the rest of the year, the bulls live in smaller all-male herds or roam by themselves.

The great slaughter

Two hundred years ago, these great animals had few enemies. Packs of wolves sometimes preyed on the weak and sickly ones. Bison were also hunted by the Plains Indians, but these hunters did not kill very many.

When the white settlers moved west, they wanted to farm the land on which the bison grazed. They did not want to compete for space with the bison, so they killed millions of these animals with rifles. The bison could not escape these powerful weapons.

Help for the bison

By 1890, there were fewer than 1,000 bison left in North America. This worried conservation-minded people who demanded that special parks and reserves be set up to save these animals. Their plans worked. Today about 50,000 bison can be found in parks and ranches in Canada and the United States. Saving the bison gives us hope that other endangered animals can also grow in number again.

Height: 77-114 inches (195-290 centimeters)
Length: 150 inches (381 centimeters)
Weight: Female: 1,200 pounds (544 kilograms)
Male: 1,800 pounds (816 kilograms)
Where it lives: The plains of North America

Bison belong to the ox family. They have hoofs, horns, and chew their cud. Camel, moose, and hippopotamuses also belong to the larger group of hoofed animals to which the bison belongs.

The prairie dog

In several parks throughout the western United States, it is possible to walk through prairie-dog towns. If you had a chance to visit one, you would be amazed! Everywhere you looked, you would see hundreds of little prairie dogs feeding on grass or popping their heads out of tunnels called **burrows**.

What are prairie dogs?

Prairie dogs are not dogs at all. They belong to the squirrel family. They were given their name by the pioneers who thought their yelps sounded like the barks of dogs.

Many colonies in one town

Colonies of related prairie dogs live next to one another in a prairie-dog town. A typical colony is made up of several families. Each family has its own burrow where the prairie dogs sleep, raise their young, and escape from their many predators, such as coyotes, badgers, bobcats, snakes, hawks, and eagles.

Where are the towns now?

In the past, a billion prairie dogs may have lived in one prairie-dog town, but as people began farming the land, they plowed under the towns and killed the prairie dogs. For some years, these chubby squirrels faced the danger of becoming extinct, but the same parks that saved the bison helped save these tiny animals, too. In the United States, quite a few parks provide homes for prairie dogs, but in Canada there is only one small prairie-dog town left. It is in a new national park in southern Saskatchewan that has been set up to save them.

Length: 11-13 inches (28-33 centimeters)
Weight: 2-3 pounds (about 1 kilogram)
Where it lives: Central North America

A single male claims up to two or three groups of related female prairie dogs as his mates. He is the protector of these females, who are believed to be sisters. The females do not allow unrelated females into the area and will chase them away. The male chases away other males until a stronger male is able to scare him away.

The kangaroo

When you think of Australia, you probably think of kangaroos. There are at least 45 different kinds of kangaroos found on this southern continent. They range from the tiny rat kangaroo to the large gray kangaroos that stand as tall as a person and can leap 27 feet (8 meters) in a single bound! Although most kangaroos are grazers and browsers and stay on the ground, there are some kangaroos that actually live in trees!

A special type of mammal

All kangaroos belong to a family of mammals called **marsupials**. Like all mammals, they have hair, are warm-blooded, and produce milk for their young. Most mammals belong to a group known as **placental** mammals. This means that the mother mammal keeps her baby inside her body until the baby is well developed.

Marsupial babies develop in a slightly different way. Mother kangaroos give birth to one baby very soon after they become pregnant. The newborn kangaroo, called a **joey**, resembles a hairless baby mouse. It must crawl up the outside of its mother's furry belly and into her pouch. Inside the pouch, the joey finds one of the mother's four nipples, to which it attaches itself. Through the nipple, it receives its mother's milk, which gives it nourishment for growing and developing.

A concern for all kangaroos

People are concerned about the survival of some species of kangaroos. The larger ones are being shot by ranchers and farmers because they share the land with cattle. The landowners do not want their cattle to have to compete for food with the kangaroos.

Each year thousands of the larger kangaroos are also killed for their hides. Their meat is used to make dog food. If this kind of slaughter goes on much longer, kangaroos will soon be threatened with extinction.

There is a concern for other types of kangaroos, too. They are called **wallabies**. *These kangaroo relatives are losing the grasslands and forests in which they live.*

Length: 15-120 inches (38-305 centimeters)
Weight: 18 ounces to 150 pounds (510 grams-68 kilograms)
Where it lives: Australia, New Zealand, New Guinea, and the nearby islands

Kangaroos have large ears and small mouths. They have long, thin, powerful hindlegs for jumping. Their tails, which are also quite long, are thick at the base to help the animals balance. Kangaroos use their front legs as arms. Their toes have sharp claws.

The cheetah

The cheetah is a perfect running machine. It has a streamlined body and powerful legs. Its long tail helps it turn rapidly without losing balance. The cheetah is the fastest land animal in the world. It can run 68 miles (110 kilometers) per hour.

A specialized cat

The cheetah is a member of the cat family, but it is considered a specialized cat. Unlike all other cats, the cheetah cannot **retract**, or pull in, its claws. Nor can a cheetah climb trees. Its long legs prevent it from doing so.

All the cheetahs of the world are very similar, and the more they breed, the more alike they become. Scientists are afraid that if the cheetah's world changes very much, this wild cat will not be able to change with it. Specialized animals such as the cheetah seem to be the first animals to become extinct because, in the wild, only the strongest and fittest animals are able to stay alive.

Hunting its own food

Cheetahs are **predators**; they eat meat. Many predators are also **scavengers** that steal meat from prey they did not kill themselves. Cheetahs, on the other hand, only eat meat from animals they have hunted. Because cheetahs have thin bones that break easily, they cannot risk fighting while scavenging. The cheetah would not be able to win a fight with a lion or hyena. That is why it must kill its own food.

Baby cheetahs

Cheetahs can have up to five babies in a litter. When a mother cheetah goes hunting, she must leave her babies. Sometimes other predators find the babies and eat them. When cheetah babies are old enough, their mother takes them hunting. Because they are so playful, they often spoil the hunt by moving around and making noise just as their mother is sneaking up on her prey.

Captive cheetahs

In the past, cheetahs were killed for their beautiful spotted fur, which was made into coats. Today few wild cheetahs are hunted, but their chances of survival are, nevertheless, not good. They are losing their habitats to farms and cities and facing the danger of extinction. Even their chance of survival in zoos is not good. Most wild cats are able to adapt to life in captivity, but cheetahs do not breed well in zoos.

Height: 32 inches (81 centimeters)
Length: (with tail) 70-86 inches (178-218 centimeters)
Weight: 86-140 pounds (39-64 kilograms)
Where it lives: Africa, southern Asia, and the Middle East

Most cheetahs now live in Africa. Although they once also lived in India, they are now extinct there. For many years, they were hunted for their beautiful fur. Their gold-colored spotted coats camouflage them well against the grasses and plants of the grasslands.

The African wild dog

The African wild dog is rapidly vanishing from most of the area in which it used to live. Once it was a common predator on the plains and savannas in Africa, but today it is a rare sight. Why? The number of African wild dogs has dropped greatly because of a disease called **rabies** and because people are their worst enemy.

A different way of hunting

Many people dislike wild dogs because of the way they hunt. Lions and cheetahs strangle their prey, but wild dogs often bite and then eat an animal while it is still alive. Even though this method of hunting is natural for wild dogs, it upsets some people. In the past, hunters killed wild dogs because people judged them to be "bad" animals.

A social animal

Today we know that there is no such thing as a "bad" animal. All animals simply follow natural ways. In fact, wild dogs could be considered very cooperative animals. They are caring parents that share their food, not only with their pups, but with other members of the pack. The aunts and uncles of the pack help raise the pups. Wild dogs are social animals that play with one another and spend time together.

An important predator

The animals killed by wild dogs are often the weak or sick ones. By killing the weak members of a herd, wild dogs actually help their prey stay healthy. The dogs also help control the number of animals in a herd. They prevent overpopulation and, in this way, ensure that there is enough food for all the herd members. Wild dogs are an important part of nature.

Equipped for a long chase

Unlike cheetahs and other cats, wild dogs can chase their prey for long distances. Cats are built for short bursts of speed. They have narrow chests with small lungs. As a result, cats quickly get out of breath and feel tired because they are unable to get all the air they need. Dogs cannot run as fast as cats, but they have bigger chests and lungs and can run much farther and longer. This means that when a wild dog starts a chase, it has a much better chance of catching its prey than a lion does because it can keep up the chase much longer.

Killer sicknesses

Wild dogs get diseases such as rabies. If one dog gets sick, the disease quickly spreads to the rest of the pack. As a result, few members of the pack stay alive. Today there are fewer than 10,000 wild dogs left in all of Africa.

Height: 30 inches (76 centimeters)
Length: 42-56 inches (107-142 centimeters)
Weight: 44-60 pounds (20-27 kilograms)
Where it lives: South of the Sahara Desert in Africa

The burrowing owl

People expect to see owls nesting or roosting in trees—not on or under the ground! There is one owl, however, that does both. It is the burrowing owl.

Nesting in grassy areas

Burrowing owls choose the abandoned burrows of ground squirrels, prairie dogs, badgers, or foxes as their homes. These tunnels provide a perfect shelter because these little owls like to nest in grassy areas. If they need to dig their own burrows, they are able to do so. Burrowing owls nest in colonies of up to a dozen pairs.

Having little owls

When burrowing owls nest, they go to the very end of the burrow, which may extend 10 feet (3 meters) from the entrance. There the female lays up to ten eggs. After the young hatch and are strong enough to climb up to the edge of the burrow, they stand there looking out at the grassland around them.

Hunting at dusk and dawn

Burrowing owls feed mainly on insects, especially grasshoppers, as well as other small creatures such as birds and mice. Their favorite hunting times are around sunrise and sunset, but sometimes they also hunt during the day. When these owls hunt, they perch on fence posts so they can hear their prey move. Once they have spotted their target, they do not fly after it. Using their long legs, they chase their prey on the ground.

A threatened species

In some parts of their range, burrowing owls are threatened and even classed as endangered. As more and more grassland is turned into farmland, there is less and less suitable land for burrowing owls. Another reason burrowing owls are threatened is that the chemical pesticides used on many farms have killed the grasshoppers that form a large part of their diets. Lastly, these small owls are an easy target for the pet dogs and cats from nearby farms.

> **Height**: 10 inches (25 centimeters)
> **Where it lives**: Southwestern Canada, western United States and Florida, Central and South America

Young burrowing owls like to stand at the edge of their burrow and look around. Their brown spotted feathers hide them well among the grasses of the plains.

The sandhill crane

The sandhill crane is looking for nesting material.

Each spring, sandhill cranes begin their flights north to their nesting grounds in the northern United States, Canada, and Alaska. They are graceful birds that fly with their necks stretched straight out. They travel in a V-formation with other birds in the sky. Some make journeys of nearly 3,500 miles (5633 kilometers) before reaching a nesting site.

Making a nest

Cranes like to nest on muskrat homes in prairie ponds. If they cannot find a nesting site, the mother and father make one. Both cranes work hard at gathering up clumps of vegetation until the nest is well above the water level. Then the female lays two or three eggs. She does not lay them at the same time. The first is laid three days before the second. If there is not enough food for both, only the older chick will survive.

Preferring plants

Although sandhill cranes eat insects, frogs, snakes, and fish, they seem to prefer plants. They like water plants in the summer, but during their flights south in the fall, they look for leftover corn, wheat, and oats in the farm fields. In the past, they were hunted when they came near a farmer's field. Today, farmers are no longer allowed to hunt them, so these birds remain safe during their long journeys.

Fewer nesting sites

The number of cranes is dropping due to a lack of nesting sites. Most of the prairie ponds that the sandhill crane used for nesting have been turned into grain fields. Fewer nests mean fewer cranes.

> **Height**: 34-48 inches (86-122 centimeters)
> **Weight**: 12 pounds (5 kilograms)
> **Where it lives**: From Alaska south to the central United States

The sandhill crane has long legs and a very long beak. It uses the beak to find plants, fish, and frogs as it stalks about the marshes. Sandhill cranes are in danger because there are fewer nesting sites for them each year. People are taking over the habitats of these birds.

The red wolf

The red wolf is one of the rarest predators in the world. It became extinct in the wild in the 1980s, and only a very few have survived in zoos. At one time, the red wolf could be found across the south-western United States and Gulf Coast, but that changed as more and more people moved onto its territories. The wolves were shot and poisoned, but that is not the reason for their near-extinction. Red wolves almost became another animal!

Despite its name, the red wolf may have a dark yellow, black, or red coat. Red wolves are smaller than other wolves.

Producing crossbreeds

As more and more wolves were killed, the ones that remained started mating with coyotes. Their pups were healthy, but they were neither coyotes nor red wolves. They were **crossbreeds**. These crossbreeds then mated with coyotes as well—as did their pups, and so on, and so on. Each time new babies were born, they were more like coyotes and less like red wolves.

Returning to the wild

Producing offspring from parents that are not similar is called **hybridization**. By the time scientists realized that the hybridization of red wolves and coyotes was taking place, there were very few true red wolves left. The few that were found were taken to zoos where they were bred with one another. By then, no wild red wolves could be found, and the species was thought to be extinct in the wilderness. Scientists thought of returning the pups to the wild, but first they had to find areas where no coyotes lived. Now, once again, a few red wolves are running free in the wilderness!

Height: 15-16 inches (38-41 centimeters)
Length: (with tail) 70-81 inches (178-206 centimeters)
Weight: 31-81 pounds (14-37 kilograms)
Where it lives: South-central United States

The red wolf almost became extinct as a species because people interfered with its natural ways and forced it to stay alive by mating with coyotes.

Preserving grasslands

If you think back to the ten animals you have just read about, you will see that there are several reasons why they were threatened with extinction. Bison and wild dogs were overhunted, red wolves nearly became coyotes, white rhinos were killed for money, and the habitats of the others are continually being destroyed.

White rhinos are guarded so that poachers will not kill them for their horns.

What is habitat destruction?

Habitat destruction means that the **ecosystem** on which an animal depends has been, or is being, destroyed. An ecosystem is a community of plants and animals and the surroundings in which they live. An ecosystem offers all the things a plant or animal needs such as good air, sunshine, fresh water, food, and soil in which plants can grow.

This picture shows how cities are taking over wilderness areas where huge herds of animals once grazed. As the human population grows, it is more difficult for wild animals to stay alive.

If a grassland ecosystem were wetter, it would become a forest; if it were drier, it would turn into a desert. If it were farmed, it would become farmland that is good for cattle but not for wildlife.

Write, talk, and visit!

You can show that you value wild areas by writing letters to your elected representatives. Tell them that you want grasslands preserved for wildlife.

Talk about why it is important to preserve endangered animals. Tell people why you would not buy products made from endangered species.

Visiting a grassland area and seeing the wildlife that inhabit it will help you understand the importance of preserving these areas. People who visit these regions also provide the grassland residents with ways of making money.

The people of the grasslands

The most important way people can help grassland animals is to make sure that grasslands remain grasslands. One of the reasons that grasslands change is that the people near them do not have enough food to eat. The result is that the grasslands are turned into farmlands.

To protect the wild grasslands, a way must be found to help feed the people who live on or near these areas. You cannot feed the world, but you can support other people's efforts to do so.

Learn all you can

You can read more about grasslands and their wildlife. Watch television shows about them. The more you know, the more you will be able to help. If everyone knew a little more, cared a little more, it would add up to a great big change. So, learn more and tell somebody else. Remember! One person can make a big difference. That person could be you!

The Masai live in East Africa and share the grasslands with wild animals. They are also finding it more difficult to survive because there is not enough grazing land for their cattle.

Glossary

antelope An animal that chews cud and has unbranched horns and split hoofs

badger An animal with a heavy body, short legs, long claws, and a short, thick tail that lives in a hole in the ground

burrow A hole dug in the ground by an animal in which it lives and hides

camouflage An animal's behavior or appearance that hides it by making it blend into its surroundings

colony A group of animals of the same kind that live together

conservation Protection from loss, harm, or waste, especially of natural resources, such as wildlife

crossbreed The offspring of the breeding of two different kinds of animals

cud The barely chewed food some animals bring up from their first stomach back into their mouth for a thorough second chewing

distress A condition of danger or need

endangered Threatened with extinction

grazer An animal that feeds on grass

habitat The natural environment of a plant or animal

hybridization Production of offspring from parents that are not similar

keratin A tough, fiberlike protein in horns, hoofs, nails, feathers, and hair

litter Young animals born at one time

marsupial A family of mammals whose females have a pouch in which the young are carried after birth

Masai A nomadic people of East Africa that raise cattle

North Yemen A country in southwestern Asia on the Red Sea

overpopulation Too many people or animals

pampas Treeless plains in South America

pesticide A chemical used to kill insects that is harmful to animals

placental A family of mammals whose females keep their young inside their bodies until the babies are well developed

poacher A person who hunts illegally

predator An animal that captures and eats other animals

prey An animal hunted by another animal for food

rabies A disease that attacks the central nervous system in warm-blooded animals. It is usually passed on by the bite of a rabid animal.

reserve Land set aside by the government for a special purpose

savanna A broad, grassy, treeless plain

scavenger An animal that feeds on decaying plants or animals

specialized Adapted to a particular environment

species A group of related plants or animals that can produce young together

steppe A broad, grassy plain in Europe or Asia

territory Any area that an animal considers its own

tradition Knowledge or customs handed down from one generation to another

unique Unusual, rare, or noteworthy

veld Open grassland in southern Africa

Index

3 4 5 6 7 8 9 0 Printed in USA 1 0 9 8 7 6 5 4 3